BONJOUR!
Let's Learn French
Visit New Places and Make New Friends!

by Judy Martialay

PoliglotKidz Press

To Ruthie, Chloé, Arjun, Axel, Eito, Eiga, Marco, Luca, Benjy, Leah Rose, Gali, Adam, and their generation.
May you love languages.

Please go to Audio Page at http://www.polyglotkidz.com to download the audio version.

Polyglotkidz Press, Sea Cliff, N.Y.
ISBN 978-0-9974687-0-0
Text and illustrations copyright© 2017 by Judy Martialay
Editor: Susan Korman
Editor for French: Isabelle Barth
Library of Congress Control Number: 2017909935

CONTENTS

Bonjour !

Hello, children! **Bonjour, les enfants !** My name is Pete the Pilot. I travel around the world and visit many countries. I have friends in these countries. I try to learn the language that they speak. People appreciate it when I speak in their language.

Today we're going to France. We're going to meet some French children. When they go to the beach, French kids love to play in the sand and water, just as we do in our country. Other activities may be new to us. Discovering the differences and similarities among people is part of the fun of traveling to another country!

Let's learn about our new friends' country, France, and their language, French.

We're going to travel by plane to France. We will land at the beach **la plage**. Please bring your bathing suit and your sunscreen.

We're getting ready to take off. Fasten your safety belts.
Here are some important words that you can learn while we're
on the plane. That way you'll be ready to meet our new friends.

Have a good trip! **Bon voyage !**

Hello   **Bonjour**
How are you? **Ça va ?**
Very well **Très bien**
And you? **Et toi ?**
Please **S'il te plaît**
Thank you very much **Merci beaucoup**
Good-bye **Au revoir**
Yes **Oui**
No **Non**
My name is (Peter) **Je m'appelle (Pierre)**.

one **un**
two **deux**
three **trois**
four **quatre**
five **cinq**

Louis, l'escargot

"Arlette, bring more water!"

Arlette runs to the water's edge, where the waves roll onto the
shore, foamy and bubbly. The sea is a bright blue **bleu** under the
summer sun. It's a beautiful day at the beach **à la plage**. There
is a boat **un bateau** in the distance.

Arlette scoops up water with her pail to mix with the sand. Pierre, Arlette, and the other children are making a castle **un château** out of sand **le sable**. The children pat the sand and water together to form the walls of the castle **le château**. Marie and Jacques make towers. Pierre has some toy soldiers who will stand guard on the towers, protecting **le château de sable**.

The children put the finishing touches on **le château**. They dig a ditch for the moat that will surround **le château**. Jacques fills the moat with water.

Pierre adds a bridge made of sticks.

Marie puts the French flag on **le château**. Blue, white, and red. **Bleu, blanc, rouge.** These are the colors of the French flag.

Arlette finds two empty shells and puts them together to make a throne for a king **un roi**.

"Mom **Maman !** Dad **Papa !** Look at **le château**. It is beautiful **Il est beau !** Now, all that is missing is a king **un roi**. But where is the king **Où est le roi ?**"

The children start to look around for **un roi**. Just then, **Maman** and **Papa** call, "Hurry up, children **Vite, les enfants !** Let's go home. It's dinnertime."

Night has arrived. The children have left the beach. Along comes Louis the snail **Louis, l'escargot**. He's making his way slowly through **le sable** looking for a comfortable place to spend the night. He sees **le château. Il est beau !** He crosses the bridge over the moat and enters **le château**. "It's perfect **C'est parfait !**

"I feel like **un roi** in his **château**. In fact, I'm going to be **le roi** of this **château !**

"King Louis, that's me **le Roi Louis, c'est moi**. I'm going to sit on that throne."

Le Roi Louis makes himself comfortable on his throne of shells. It's dinnertime, and Louis is getting hungry. **Un roi** can order whatever he pleases.

"Onion soup, please **La soupe à l'oignon, s'il vous plaît !** I love onion soup **J'adore la soupe à l'oignon !**"

Louis waits for his royal dinner to arrive.

Suddenly, he hears loud noises. **Ouah, ouah, grrr. Miaou, miaou, grrr. Bijou,** the dog **le chien**, is barking and chasing **Chou Chou,** the cat **le chat**.

They don't see **le beau château**. They run right over it and don't even look back!

Le château, the flag, the towers, the soldiers, and the bridge have all fallen down. Oh, my goodness **Oh là là** ! The castle is in ruins!

Poor Louis **Pauvre Louis !** His dream of being **le Roi Louis** is gone.

"Where will I spend the night? My throne is in pieces. I'll have to sleep on the floor. That's life **C'est la vie !**

"Oh, well, it isn't so bad. I can sleep in my own shell. Maybe I'm not the king, but I am Louis the snail **Je suis Louis, l'escargot**. We snails have our shells to sleep in."

Zzz . . . zzz. . . zzz . . .

The next day, the children return to the beach. "**Oh, là, là ! Le château** is in ruins! That's a shame **C'est dommage !**"

They see Louis asleep in **le château** on the floor in his shell. "Poor Louis **Pauvre Louis !**"

Jacques has an idea. "Louis, we've been looking for **un roi** for our castle, and you are **le roi parfait**. We're going to rebuild **le château** for you."

The children work hard. They make piles of sand and fetch pails of water. They put back the towers, the toy soldiers, the throne made of shells, the moat, the bridge, and the flag. And there, **voilà !** Once again **le château est beau**. **C'est parfait !**

Everyone shouts, "Long live King Louis L'Escargot **Vive le Roi Louis, l'escargot !**"

Le Roi Louis thanks the children for his **château**. "**Merci beaucoup, les enfants !**"

C'est à toi ! *It's Your Turn!*

Bonjour !

Imagine that you are at the beach **à la plage**, *introducing yourself to Arlette, Pierre, Jacques, and Marie. Here's what you can say:*

Bonjour ! Je m'appelle *(your name).* Hi! My name is (your name).

Et toi ? And you?

You can also say: **Tu t'appelles comment ?** What's your name?
Introduce yourself to your friends and family. Then ask them their names.

Ça va?

To ask your friend, How are you?, you can say **Ça va ?**

Here's how Louis answers:

très bien   **bien**   **comme ci, comme ça**   **mal**

Ça va, Louis ?

Ça va très mal !

Et toi ? Ça va ? *Give your answer!*

Now, ask your friends and family **Ça va ?**

Des gens et des choses *People and Things*

Here are some new words. Can you guess what they mean?*

un vélo   **un ballon**   **un garçon**   **une fille**

une voiture   **un drapeau**   **une fleur**   **un arbre**

**a bicycle, a ball, a boy, a girl, a car, a flag, a flower, a tree*

Où est . . .? *Where is . . .?*

Where can you find these people and things? You may find some in all three places!

À la plage at the beach   **à l'école** at school   **à la maison** at home

un ballon
un oignon
une fille

une fleur
le sable
un drapeau

un garçon
un escargot
un bateau

La chasse au trésor *Treasure Hunt*

Look for these people and things inside and outside of your home. Can you find them? **Oui ou non** *yes or no?*

un chien
un chat
un roi
un bateau
un enfant
trois oignons
un garçon

un drapeau
quatre fleurs
une fille
un escargot
deux ballons
un vélo
cinq arbres

Which ones did you find?

Here's how to point out people and things when you see them.
Use **voici** *and* **voilà**.
Voici *Here is/are . . .*
Voilà *There is/are . . .*

Voici une fleur. *Here is a flower.*
Voici deux fleurs. *Here are two flowers.*
Voilà un garçon. *There is a boy.*
Voilà deux garçons. *There are two boys.*

Coloriez le monde *Color the World*

Voici les couleurs. *Here are the words for some colors:*

| bleu | blanc | rouge | vert |

| jaune | noir | orange | marron |

Find objects in your house with these colors and name the color. For example:
the wall: **blanc**
a coat: **marron**

Quelle est la couleur ? *What Is the Color?*

Can you name the colors on this artist's palette?

Bravo !

Test de couleur *Color Quiz*

Which colors can you name in this picture of Colmar, France?

Super!

L'expression du jour *Daily Expression*

Here's an expression for each day of the week. Try to use each expression several times during each day. Mark how many times you use that expression in the chart below. For example, if you use **J'adore !** *three times on* **lundi** *Monday, write the number 3.*

J'adore !

C'est parfait !

C'est dommage !

S'il te plaît ! *

Oh là là !

C'est la vie !

Merci beaucoup !

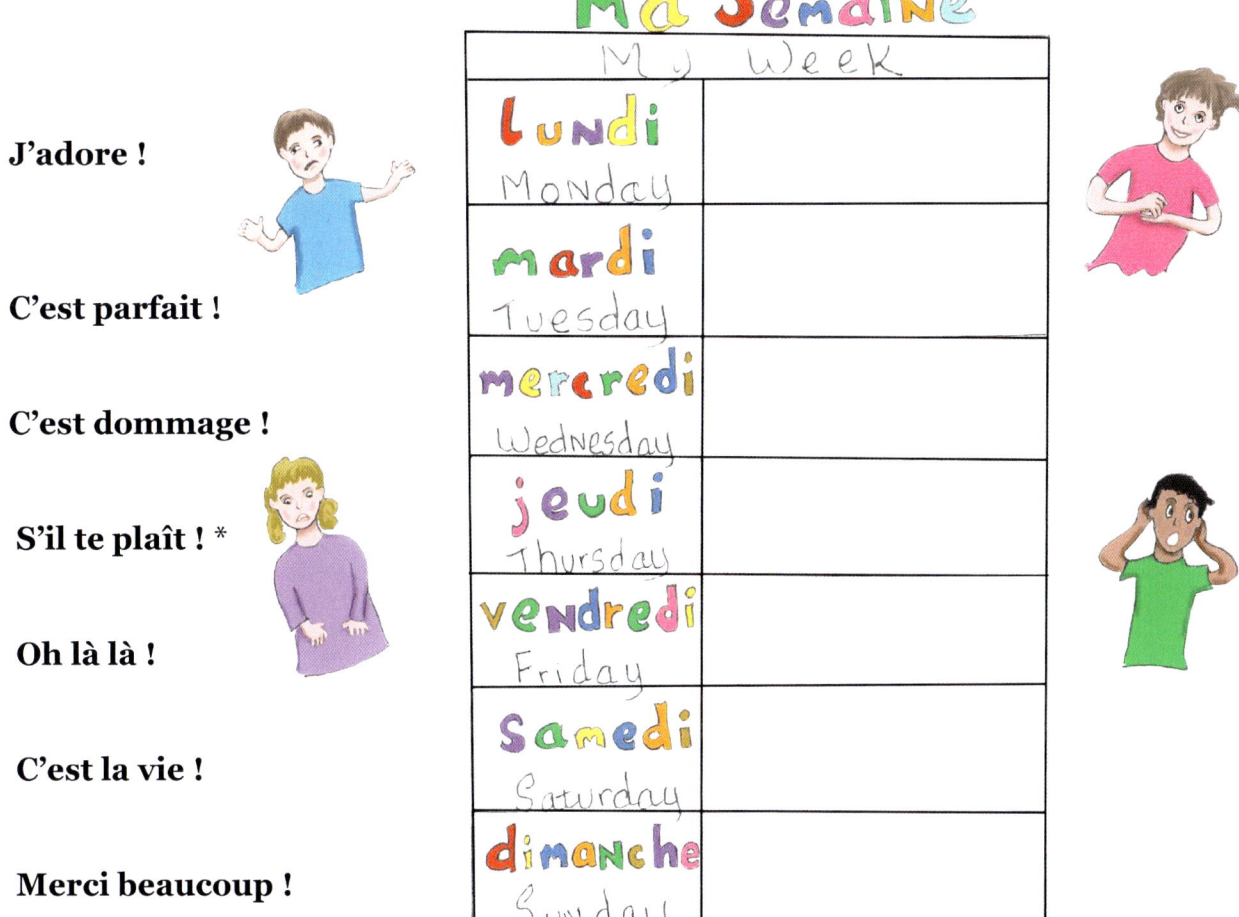

Ma Semaine	
My Week	
Lundi Monday	
mardi Tuesday	
mercredi Wednesday	
jeudi Thursday	
vendredi Friday	
Samedi Saturday	
dimanche Sunday	

Use **s'il te plaît** *when you talk to a child, a teenager, a family member, or a grown-up who is a close friend of the family. Use* **s'il vous plaît** *when you talk to an adult who is not a family member or a close friend of the family, like your teacher or a police officer. Use it when you're speaking to more than one person too.*

Louis va en ville *Louis Goes to Town*

Have fun acting out this skit with some friends. Louis and his friends are making plans for the day.

Louis:	**Bonjour, les amis !**	Louis:	Hello, friends!
Ami*:	**Bonjour, Louis.**	Friend:	Hello, Louis.
	Tu vas où ?		Where are you going?
Louis:	**Je vais en ville.**	Louis:	I'm going to town.
Ami:	**Pourquoi ?**	Friend:	Why?
Louis:	**Je vais au café.**	Louis:	I'm going to the café.
	Je vais manger un croissant.		I'm going to eat a croissant.
	J'adore les croissants.		I love croissants.
Ami:	**Moi aussi. J'adore les croissants.**	Friend:	Me too. I love croissants.
Ami:	**Moi aussi.**	Friend:	Me too.
	On va au café ensemble ?		Shall we go to the café together?
Tous:	**Super !**	Everyone:	Great!
Louis:	**On traverse la rue ?**	Louis:	Shall we cross the road?
Tous:	**Très bien.**	Everyone:	OK.
			(*Start to cross the street*)

In the skit, **ami, a male friend, is used to stand for either **un ami** or **une amie**, a female friend. There is no difference in pronunciation.*

Chauffeur de voiture: Tut, tut !	Car driver: Beep, beep!
Attention !	Watch out!
Ami: Vite, Louis !	Friend: Fast, Louis!
Cycliste: Attention !	Bicycle rider: Watch out!
Ami: Vite, Louis !	Friend: Hurry up, Louis!
Louis: C'est impossible.	Louis: It's impossible.
Je suis un escargot.	I'm a snail.
Je suis très lent.	I'm very slow.
Motocycliste: Vroum, vroum !	Motorcycle rider: (*make the roar of a motorcycle*)
Attention !	Watch out!
Amis: Oh, là, là!	Friends: Oh, no!
C'est dangereux !	It's dangerous!
Au secours !	Help!
Agent de police:	Police officer: (*walking over*)
J'arrive !	I'm coming!
(Sifflet): Stop !	(*Whistle*) Stop!
	(*Louis and his friends cross the street.*)
Tous: Merci beaucoup,	Everyone: Thank you very much,
Monsieur (ou) Madame.	sir (*or*) ma'am.

Coin de culture
Culture Corner

Le français : French is spoken regularly in almost forty countries all over the world. These countries are in Europe, Africa, North America, the Caribbean, South America, Asia, and the Pacific Islands. Countries where French is commonly spoken are called the Francophone countries. Can you name some of these countries?

La France : France is located in western Europe. Many countries border on France. Can you locate France and name its bordering countries on the map?

Les plages : France has many beaches because of its coastlines along the English Channel, the Atlantic Ocean, and the Mediterranean Sea. A favorite place for French families to vacation is at the beach **à la plage**. Kids all over the world love to build things in the sand, such as sand castles. Have you ever made **un château de sable**? What else can you make with sand?

La plage à Nice, France

Le Roi Louis : Today France has a president. Long ago, France had **les rois** kings. The most popular name for French kings was **Louis**. There were eighteen kings named **Louis**! Other kings' names were **Philippe**, **Charles**, and **François**. What name do you like for a king?

The French word for queen is **reine**. Do you know the names of any queens?

Louis XIV

Le drapeau français : The French flag has three colors: **bleu, blanc, rouge** blue, white and red. It is called **le tricolore** because of the three colors. Can you name the colors of your country's flag in French?

My flag is . . . **Mon drapeau est . . .**

La soupe à l'oignon : French onion soup has broth, onions, and is topped by a layer of crusty bread and melted cheese. It is a very comforting dish in cold weather.

Les chiens et les chats : The French enjoy having pets. They own fish, birds, and other animals, but cats and dogs are the most popular pets. Dog owners like to take their dogs to restaurants, stores, and on buses and trains. The French poodle, **le caniche**, is a popular breed.

Here are some French names for dogs and cats. Which one would you choose?

Bijou, Boumboum, Chopin, Loulou, Mirage, Moustache, Pompom, Pouding, Scoubidou

Deux caniches

Do you have a pet? Speaking to your pet in French is a great way to practice the language. Here are some commands that you can teach your dog:

Sit down **Assis !**
Give me your paw **Donne la patte !**
Stay **Reste !**

Le croissant : A **croissant** is a buttery, flaky pastry shaped like a crescent. **Le croissant** is very popular for breakfast in France. **C'est délicieux !** It's delicious!

Le café : **Les cafés** are places to have a snack, **un croissant**, and something to drink. **Les cafés** have tables inside, and outside in good weather. People like to sit and read or talk with their friends, do their work, and watch the passersby. Customers can stay for a long time in a café.

The waiter is **un garçon**. Would you like to order **un croissant**? Here's how:

Un croissant, s'il vous plait.
How would you order two croissants? Five croissants?
Deux/cinq croissants, s'il vous plait. The "s" at the end of **croissant̲s̲** is silent.

CHANSON *Song*

"Ah! Mon beau château !"
"Oh ! My Beautiful Castle!"

There are several verses to this song; just the first two are included here. It can be sung in rounds or all at once.

Première ronde:
Ah ! Mon beau château !
Ma tant', tire, lire, lire,
Ah ! Mon beau château !
Ma tant', tire, lire, lo.

First verse:
Oh! My beautiful castle!
(sounds, no meaning)
Oh! My beautiful castle!
(sounds)

Deuxième ronde:
Le nôtre est plus beau,
Ma tant', tire, lire, lire,
Le nôtre est plus beau,
Ma tant', tire, lire, lo.

Second verse:
Ours is more beautiful,
(sounds)
Ours is more beautiful.
(sounds)

Faisons un dessin impressionniste

Let's Make an Impressionist Picture

Have you ever noticed how shadows change throughout the day, or how trees and branches sway in the wind? How the clouds move through the sky and change shape? Two centuries ago, a group of artists in France painted the changes that they saw in the world around them: the motion of water, wind, the sun shining on the grass or the water, the clouds moving rapidly or lazily through the sky. They wanted to capture their *impressions* of their surroundings as they painted; these artists became known as impressionists. Their paintings are among the best-loved in the world.

Claude Monet: The Artist's Garden at Vetheuil

We're going to make some impressionist-style pictures using oil pastels or crayons. Just follow these steps. They're as easy as **un, deux, trois !**

1. Outline the shapes in your drawing lightly with a regular pencil. No details necessary.
2. Color your picture with basic colors. For example, for water, use blue. For a leaf, use green. For a lemon, use yellow.
3. Look at the color wheel below. Find the colors that you just used. Look at the colors next to these, and add them to your picture. For yellow, choose mostly yellow-green and yellow-orange. Then use colors farther away from your basic color, like green, orange, and other colors.

This activity should be done with adult supervision.

Un citron *A Lemon*

Let's make an impressionist picture of a lemon **un citron !** It's easy **C'est facile !** We'll use **les pastels à l'huile** oil pastels; you can also use **les crayons cire** crayons. You may want to try both and see which one you like better. See the special notes for using crayons.

This is a good time to review the colors in French. Do you remember them? **Les couleurs : bleu blanc rouge vert jaune noir orange marron.** Consult page 17 if you need to review.

If you are using oil pastels for your picture, you will need:

- a lemon
- a set of oil pastels
- strong paper like "paper for all media"
- some paper towels
- a pencil
- a good eraser
- old newspapers to protect the work area

1. Draw the shape of the lemon lightly with a regular pencil. Include the stem if you see one.

2. Color the lemon with its main color, yellow. If part of the lemon is in the shade, use ochre for a darker yellow. For the lightest part of the lemon, use white with yellow.

Tip: With oil pastels, it's best to apply the lightest colors first. Try out the colors on a piece of scrap paper.

3. Now, using the color wheel, add the colors that are to the right and left of yellow: yellow-green, green, yellow orange, orange and orange-red. Add yellow-orange and orange in the lightest parts. Many lemons have a bit of green. So you can add some light green. To show shaded parts of the lemon, add some green and blue.

4. Keep adding more of these colors. You may blend the colors with your finger.

5. To show the shadow that the lemon makes on the table, use purple or violet and blue.

Tip: Keep your pastels clean with a paper towel.

For a crayon drawing, you will need:
- a lemon
- pencil
- eraser
- paper
- crayons

1. Draw the outline of the lemon in pencil.

2. Color the lemon with its main color, yellow. If you see shade or a stem, use a darker yellow (ochre) and a little brown. Don't color too heavily.

3. Follow steps #3 and #5 above.

4. Unlike with oil pastels, you cannot blend with crayon. At the end, you may want to color more heavily, but don't break the crayon!

Tip: Crayons often come with mixed colors: blue-green, orange-yellow. Try out the colors on a scrap paper before you use them. Your crayons may have the colors written in French!

Voilà ! Write the title **Un citron** *A Lemon* on the bottom of your picture and sign it.

You can also make a picture of a banana, **une banane**, in crayon or oil pastels following the steps above.

Now you can try other pictures: Some of the pictures below are painted in oil pastel; others are colored with crayons.

un arbre a tree

une fleur a flower

des fruits fruits

un bateau a boat

Tout ! Everything and anything!

Amuse-toi ! Have fun!

Les mots   Words

These are the words that are introduced in the book, organized by chapter:

BONJOUR

Au revoir ! Good-bye!
Bon voyage ! Have a good trip!
Bonjour ! Hello! (during the day)
Bonsoir ! Good evening!
Ça va ? How are you?
cinq five
deux two
un enfant a child
les enfants the children
Et toi ? And you?
Je m'appelle . . . My name is . . .

Merci beaucoup ! Thank you very much!
non no
oui yes
la plage the beach
quatre four
s'il te plaît please (for people you know well)
s'il vous plaît please (polite and plural)
très bien very well
trois three

LOUIS, L'ESCARGOT

à la plage at the beach
un bateau a boat
beau beautiful
blanc white
bleu blue
C'est dommage. It's a pity.
C'est la vie. That's life.
C'est parfait. It's perfect.
un chat a cat
un château a castle
un château de sable a sand castle
le chien the dog
un escargot a snail
Il est . . . It is. . . (he is)
J'adore . . . I love . . . I am fond of . . .

je suis . . . I am . . .
Maman Mom
Oh là, là ! Oh, my!
Où est . . . ? Where is . . . ?
Papa Dad
pauvre poor
un roi a king
le roi the king
rouge red
le sable the sand
la soupe à l'oignon onion soup
vite fast
Vive. . . ! Long live . . .!
Voilà . . . There is/are . . .
Voilà ! There!

C'EST À TOI

à l'école at school
à la maison at home
un ami a male friend
une amie a female friend
un arbre a tree
Attention ! Watch out!
au café to the café
Au secours ! Help!
un ballon a ball
Bravo ! Bravo! Hurray! Great!
C'est dangereux. It's dangerous.
C'est impossible. It's impossible
Ça va bien. I'm fine.
comme ci, comme ça so-so
les couleurs the colors
un croissant a croissant
un drapeau a flag
en ville to town
ensemble together
une fille a girl
une fleur a flower
un garçon a boy
J'arrive. I'm coming.
jaune yellow
Je vais. I'm going

lent slow
les the, before a plural noun
les croissants the croissants
mal bad
manger to eat
marron brown
Moi aussi. Me too.
noir black
On traverse. Let's cross.
On va ? Shall we go?
orange orange
Pourquoi ? Why?
la rue the street
Super ! Great! Awesome!
Tu t'appelles comment ? What's your name?
Tu vas où ? Where are you going?
un vélo a bicycle
vert green
vite fast
Voici . . . Here is . . .
Voilà . . . There is . . .
une voiture a car

COIN DE CULTURE

Assis ! Sit down!
le café the coffee shop
C'est délicieux ! It's delicious!
une chanson a song
les châteaux the castles
Donne la patte ! Give me your paw!

Le français French (language)
La France France
un garçon a waiter
une reine a queen
Reste ! Stay!

FAISONS UN DESSIN IMPRESSIONNISTE

Amuse-toi ! Have fun!
C'est facile. It's easy.
un citron a lemon
un crayon cire a crayon
des fruits some fruit
un pastel à l'huile an oil pastel
tout everything

MERCI BEAUCOUP!

Thank you so much to my dear friends and colleagues whose encouragement and advice helped me to make this book possible.

Harriet Barnett
Kokila Bennet, music consultant
Lisa Giurlando, art consultant
Rosemary Haigh

Tachy Houillier
Michele Pollard
Babeth Jarin-Scheiner, audio recording
Louise Terry

Photo credits

Colmar, France: Janoka 82
Palette: Krasyuk
Map of France: omersukrugoksu
Beach in Nice, France: MariaMarcone
French castle, Chateau comtal
Carcassonne: andy 2673
French flag: Ramberg
Onion soup: LauriPatterson
Poodles: gronimo

Croissant: ermingut
Woman reading book in Paris café: encrier
Waiter: paparazzit
Portrait of Louis XIV: Everett-art
Monet painting 1880, *The Artist's Garden at Vetheuil*: Everett-Art
Color wheel: litu92458
Lavender in Provence: sara-winter

Audio credit
Spring in Paris 02 by Pedro duvall/ Pond5.com